London to Chester

and back

by narrowboat

© Richard Monkhouse 2014.   All rights reserved.
Published by AHA! PRESS UK
Edition 1, 17/11/20

The word 'flattle' as canal slang does not appear in the dictionary, but I am one, living part time in a house, and part time on a boat. I have owned my narrowboat 'Moonstone' for eighteen years, keeping her near Uxbridge, and although travelling much of the canal system in the south, I had never ventured far north of Northampton. Midsummer had come and gone and many of my friends were away, so as self employed and part retired, a break of six weeks was possible, and it became evident that now was the time to go. I chose Chester because I had been told that the Shropshire Union canal was worth the journey.

Day 1. Friday 27th June 2014,

I take a taxi to Willowtree Marina just three miles away. Nearing the approach my heart sinks as I realise that I have left the keys to the marina gate on the boat. Untypically for this time of the morning however, the gate is open.

Moonstone is stocked up ready, and I set straight off at 7:30am. Ten minutes down the Paddington arm towards Southall, I pass residential boats with well kept waterside gardens. Under Southall bridge and coming the other way along the towpath, a dishevelled sikh is talking on his phone, followed by a brown gundog and a female cyclist, as I pass Minit Island down to Bulls Bridge junction.

The sky is brighter and it is warm at 18°C, although rain is forecast.

I treat myself to the luxury of breakfast at Tesco's. Audrey Hepburn isn't there, although a beautiful Polish waitress dishes out my eggs and bacon.

Our own poles of madness are like the still point where there is no wind, or the point on the head from which hair radiates. The wind or hair are like our awareness, and there has inevitably to be some point where the hair or wind cease. Our own personal view of the world must inevitably have a blind spot. Being on a boat is a form of meditation, a chance to mend the angst of daily existence.

I pass the Slough canal arm at 10:07am. A Dutch barge has self-enforced its residential status as its enlarged wheel house is now built around the lowered mast. I pass the 'Waters Edge' restaurant, previously the 'Turning Point', and under Packet Boat Lane Bridge, past another new Tesco supermarket opposite a housing estate which once used to be a bitumen factory.

Tame blue Damsel flies flirt with the cream boat roof. A small beautiful wildflower meadow grabs my attention from behind the towpath nearing Cowley lock at 10:30am where volunteer lock keepers speed me through this first of the forty-one uphill locks to the Tring summit.

I pass narrowboat 'Hippo'. It had been tarred pitch black for the last decade, but now to my surprise is painted red. I get through 'Uxbridge' lock, then a steady pace through the suburban parkland and the locks named, 'Denham Deep', 'Widewater', 'Blackjacks', 'Coppermill', 'Springwell', 'Stockers', 'Batchworth' and 'Lot Mead'.

Finally there is hot sun, blue sky, though a cool breeze. I clear 'Common Moor' lock just before Croxley Green at 5pm. Now is the pedestrian rush hour. I am relieved to get a text from friend Kannicha, to say that she has got to Thailand safely.

I pass under three bridges at Croxley Green. Pass 'Norton Star'. At Cassiobury a bemused Indian man with his daughter watches the cascade of water as I fill the lock. I offer a short boat ride over the ten minutes to 'Iron Bridge' lock. I think they are intrigued by the floating perspective.

In the woods beside the lock a photographer is taking pictures of a scantily-clad girl. I am through this lock at 6:15pm, then up through the two locks by the park cottage, to moor just below the pleasantly sculpted Lady Capel bridge in the grounds of the Grove House Hotel. This Hotel, a previous stately home, is a rich mans club and golf course that has recently hosted the secretive though widely publicised Bilderburg conference, a group meeting of world leaders, whose agenda has caused much suspicion amongst conspiracy theorists.

I cook a quick salmon with vegetable supper, then phone a few friends, and go to bed at 8:30pm for a well deserved sleep. I have done fifteen locks today.

Moored near Lady Capel Bridge. Moonstone is the second boat

Day 2, Saturday 28th June.

Breakfast is at 6:15am, then I walk across the Capel bridge and up to the £350 a night Grove Hotel to have a nose around. I set off at 7:50am. After Lady Capel lock, I pass a hire boat from Stone, the North Country origin of my boat. Passing through the lock at the entrance to Hunton Bridge at 8:25am. I think of the rather sad donkey that used to live on the small patch of ground between the lock and road. I pass through the second lock at 8:55am. A young blonde lady smoking a cigarette emerges from the lock keepers cottage and heads off to work.

I approach fishermen and slow down to 'tick-over' speed. The slow pace is doing me good: boat meditation practice: less is more: slower is faster. Reaching North Grove lock the sun shines. I think of this as 'electric-cable' lock as a rather dangerous looking connection joins the adjacent lock keepers cottage to a nearby pylon.

Numbered walkers jog along the towpath in a marathon all the way from Watford to Bletchley.   Here is the path of escape from London as the canal runs under, the M25.
As I pass along this stretch a brief lapse of concentration results in a near collision with a bankside tree, and in the ensuing brush of branches across the roof, I lose overboard the essential bamboo cane that I use as a fuel gauge. A few minutes are spent reversing and retrieving it.

At the next lock I chat to a man with his grand daughter. They have come out to watch the marathon. Kites – the birds of prey - are circling overhead. They have increased in number and spread dramatically since their re-introduction into the Thames valley. The Ovaltine factory, once a landmark on the canal, has now completely vanished, replaced by flats for escapee Londoners.

The marathon walkers are now passing thick and fast. Three more locks, then by 11:25am I get to Nash Mills at Apsley where I moor the boat and go into a new canalside restaurant to have a pint of weak beer and a delicious sardine snack.

I am feeling tired, and it is starting to rain. I set off through Nash Mills lock, then the pair of locks by the maintenance centre of British Waterways (now renamed the Canal and River Trust). Passing up through the first lock at Hemel Hempstead, then through Boxmoor, I reach the swing bridge at Winkwell, where its operation holds the local traffic up for a couple of minutes.

Then by some luck I pair up with another boat, usually a huge advantage when navigating up the double width locks of the Grand Union canal. It is is a time share from Warwick part owned by a couple from Ealing. The water level is so low that I cannot tie up below the next lock. We pass through the two locks above Winkwell, then through the stinky and foamy Sewer Lock, and through another lock before reaching the Rising Sun pub at the entrance to Berkhampstead. It is hosting a real ale festival. People are spread right across the lock, in which a boat has a beer driven reluctance to exit. Finally up through some more locks, past the railway station and one last lock to moor nearby a very welcome Waitrose at 7pm. Today I have done 21 locks.

The entry to Berkhampstead, by the 'Boat'.

Day 3, Sunday 29th June

I take a more leisurely morning, and after stocking up with some food from wonderful Waitrose I set off to the North of Berkhampstead at 10:20am. Clear two locks, the second is 'Gas' lock at 11:01am, then clear 'Bushes' lock at 11:22am. I have a

well deserved cup of coffee, then up to Northchurch lock where there is a pumping station, topping up the canal water. At Lock 49, the fence is being repainted by an enthusiastic canal lover. I head on up through the last lock in the flight up to Cowroast Marina where I first bought Moonstone eighteen years ago.
My friend Jock has rung and aims to meet me at Bulbourne in the afternoon. He has just got a motorbike, and is keen to demonstrate his mobility. I have known Jock from way back in time when I was at my first job migrating from mechanical design to electronics at Marconi in Borehamwood

I navigate the gorge which is the Tring summit, and find a mooring space opposite the British Waterways lock repair centre, where much of the warehouse has now been rented out.
I am hopeful that I can make a bit more progress before nightfall. I realise the necessity to achieve an 'escape velocity'! So many times in the past I have never got past Braunston – near Northampton – and I realise that if I can get there in a week or so, then I will have the resolve to navigate around Birmingham and get up to my goal on the Shropshire Union canal.

Jock finally arrives mid afternoon. After trying hard to de-program him from motorbike to canal mode, I suggest a bite of late lunch. The canalside White Lion pub is now closed, so we head a few yards down the road to the Anglers Retreat at which we get simple but tasty fare. After returning to Moonstone, Jock pulls all the stops out, and helps prepare each of the locks in turn, I descend five out of the six locks to Marsworth basin, mooring amidst the wild foul, including swans, with an open view over the nearby lakes. Today I have done only twelve locks, but I am past the summit.

Day 4, Monday the 30th June

I am up and off at 8:50am, then through the bottom Marsworth lock, and under the road bridge into a serene and tranquil basin. The canal curves around the base of the village, and I pass "Tripos" and "MaidofFibre.com".

The next two locks, 38 and 37, are on a hillside, just out of town. They have leaky gates, are empty, and take a long time to ready. I wonder whether the expression "Don't fly off the handle" came from canal folk. Certainly it is the last thing you want to happen as you lower a gate paddle, because the chances are that the handle itself will fly off the spindle, and probably it will fall directly into the water, or indirectly after a bounce on the stonework, or cause a nasty injury.

Energetic cyclists chat to me as I emerge out of the second lock at 10:10am. I pass Dunstable boat club and narrowboat "Grumpy Otter". There is a horrible swing bridge coming up, it is not designed with the solo boater in mind. I may have to moor on the swivel side of the bridge, and rope the boat around from one difficult single mooring bollard to one on the other side, and then close the bridge. This whole lengthy shenanigans is circumvented by the timely arrival of two canny walkers who see my plight, and swing the bridge open. All I have to do is chug slowly through and give them my thanks.

The section of the canal between Marsworth and Leighton Buzzard is in general well away from roads. I pass through Seabrook lock No 36 at 10:35am, and No 35 at 11:19am. At lock 33, Ivinghoe, I meet the Mikron Theatre boat coming the other way. The Mikron Theatre Company was founded in 1963 in Marsden and spends the summer touring the country by canal.

Cows crows and high voltage cables announce our passage past smelly livestock buildings. I am out of Horton lock, 31, at 12:52. Then at Slapton, No 30, I fill up with water, leaving at 1:33pm.

I consume a quick but expensive 'half' and a packet of crisps at the Grove pub by Grove lock, No 28. A BW man helps me through the lock, emerging at 2:57pm to enter the outskirts of Leighton Buzzard.

I moor by the canalside Tesco, but get supplies from Waitrose just up the high. Then I leave at 4:42pm. By the exit lock of

Leighton Buzzard, a mosquito like motor cyclist is destroying the tranquillity of a nearby corn field. A pitbull owner apologises for his dog taking a lunge at me as I open the lock gates.

Further on, just before the boat friendly Globe Inn. I pass two giant wide beam boats with large owners and large TVs. I moor and make myself a very tasty roast chicken, beetroot and potatoes with broad beans lemon, and feta cheese.

Day 5, Tuesday the 1st July

I wake from a disturbing nightmare in which I see water leaking out from behind the bulging skirting board in an upstairs room in my childhood house, Wyck Cottage in Pinner. In the waking world, my ankle is rather swollen, and my back hurts – caution is required.

I am off, past the Globe Inn, at 7:50am. The sky is blue and clear. Amidst the beautiful countryside, I pass "Isabella", and "Candy Boat". Long fast sleek eleven carriage Virgin trains pass on the nearby line. Past tough live-aboard 'pirate' boats. Into the three locks at Soulbury at 8:30am, and speedily out of the flight at 9:02am. This is quick, but I am trying to be more tortoise than hare. Past "Tegu and the Welsh Wizard".

Towards Stoke Hammond the canal is lined with tall linden trees. At the next lock I pass another boat. I am out of the lock at 9:43am, and through Fenny Stratford Garden Suburb. Through the eccentric lock by a pub, and with the swing bridge across it, and only a 6" drop at 10:50am. Rare looking elliptical lily pads adorn the waters edge. Bletchley leads into Milton Keynes. Poplar trees line the well mown grassy towpath.

I stop at 1pm, and after a disappointed inspection of a nearby pub which is obviously geared to robbing tourists who are not from the area, I make myself a lunch of cheese and spring onion sandwiches. I am off again at 1:20pm, and after 30mins I am near Bradwell, out of the gardened centre of Milton Keynes.

I pass through the lock at Cosgrove, past the Buckingham arm, through the Gothic shaped Solomon's bridge, and then moor near Grafton Regis.

I moor by some other boats, just after a bridge and start a chicken curry. I get complementary comments on the aroma from passing boats, but the mooring isn't ideal, being near to a bridge, and being bounced into the bank as boats pass. So after a walk to survey the local area, I move the boat on a short distance to a more pleasant location for the evening.

Solomon's Bridge at Cosgrove

Day 6, Wednesday the 2nd of July

I wake to a peaceful morning. There are myriads of dew drops on the wild plants by the towpath.
At last I have a relaxed water gypsy feeling now that I have got out into the countryside.
I am off at 8:30am, passing the old manor house. The canal winds by its feeder river, the 'Tove'.

A traditional boat and butty is selling gas and fuel. This is reassuring, but I don't need anything yet.

I reach the flight of five locks in the approach to Stoke Bruerne at 9:30am, and manage to complete them by 10:36am.

In the top lock just before Stoke Bruerne

I have been to this 'tourist' spot before, so I do not stop, but proceed to the two mile tunnel, entering it at 11:15am, and out at 11:56, after a good soaking from the water gushing in down the air shafts.

Nearing the exit of the Blisworth tunnel

After the tunnel I stop at Blisworth to do some shopping up the hill. Then I set off to to Bugbrooke. Well named as it is full of horse flies. Virgin trains pass me at high speed. I pass "Rosé and Gin" at low speed!

I moor at Nether Heyford between bridges 32 and 29 at 3:12pm on a pleasant bend with the town to the north. It is a Shepherds delight sunset.

Sunset at Nether Heyford

Day 7, Thursday 3rd July

I feel that I have achieved orbital speed, and it is time for a trip home. I make the short journey from Nether Heyford to Weedon Bec, and find an unlikely but safe mooring spot on the aquaduct near the bridge on the town side of the canal, away from the towpath. There I descend the wooden steps to the village and get the bus to Northampton, and then the speedy Virgin train home via Watford, followed by a taxi to the underground station, and the metropolitan line to Hillingdon and home. The journey takes about three hours.

The canal, village and church at Weedon Bec

Day 8, Friday 4th July
Back in Hillingdon I do the tedious job of gathering paperwork for my accountant.

Day 9, Saturday 5th July
It is raining, and there is no local car boot sale to provide amusement.
I think I will go back to the boat tomorrow.

Day 10, Sunday 6th July

It is a fairly easy trip back. Whilst waiting for the bus in Northampton I answer a phone call and a Russian man warns me about the health dangers of using mobile phones. I get back to Weedon Bec, and have a half in the "Feathers". I move the boat about half a mile further on under a small bridge on the outskirts of Weedon Town.

I make dinner; it is a cool 11°C outside, time for a small warming fire. The little wood burner in the boat, when ignited with some twigs and a couple of small logs, heats up quickly, and makes the lounge cosy and me happy.

Day 11, Monday 7th July

I make two trips on foot to Weedon getting milk and mustard. Up the hill back to the canal bridge there are three antique shops. Back by the canal it is busy, other boats pass! Finally I am off at 8:55am, I chase the last boat to pass, as I know there are more locks coming up. The canal takes a windy path between the railway and the road. Wooded glades have some popular isolated moorings. I am nearing Whilton, with its flight of six locks. At 10am I manage to pair up with another boat and we do the flight in two hours.

Door of cottage at the top of the Whilton flight

At the top there is a pub, and I go in for a well deserved half and a portion of chips.

I set off again at 12:30 to reach the Braunston tunnel at 1:01pm and exit at 1:31pm. I am down the Braunston flight by 2:52pm.

There are many beautifully painted 'trad' boats lining the canal, as I pass through the canal centre and head north, up the Oxford Canal for just one mile before mooring in the glorious open countryside at 3:38pm.

Moored just north of Braunston

After research with online maps, I find that I am near a prison! I walk up the beautiful rural and windy canal, under a bridge with a very noticeable acoustic echo, and through a cornfield. I see no signs of the prison. I return and go to sleep early hoping that there are no mad axmen wandering around.

Day 12, Tuesday 8th July

I am up early with breakfast at 6:30am. I check the fuel level with a bamboo stick. It registers 16.8 centimetres, which roughly translated is about 17 gallons. A full day's travel uses about a gallon. These estimates are my own folk lore, and I note down this figure with the idea of improving their accuracy.

It is misty, but with the promise of a clear blue sky. I am off at 7:30am. A rabbit, with eyes in the back of its head darts off into the hedge. I continue the search for the prison, so clear on the aerial photos on Google Earth. It is somewhere near bridge 80, its search has become an obsession. I moor, climb the bridge, see no prison, walk across the canal and up a nearby hill, still no sighting. It is clear to me now that it is there, though well hidden in a thicket of trees.

I set off again at 9:09am along 'Barby strait'. On the radio an institutional geologist is making a propagandised case for fracking and nuclear waste burial.

I reach Hillmorton town at 9:48. Under bridge 73 painted with the history of Rugby football. I reach the three locks at Hillmorton at 10:10am. Three pairs of single width locks are old and curious. No canal traffic jams here! They are quick to empty, and their double downstream exit gates easy to open. With the help of an unexpected lock-keeper, I am out of the flight at 10:10am.

To the right of the canal is a field full of wires and steel towers. This is the vast Rugby submarine communications aerial array, and no doubt was a strategic nuclear target.

Glorious buddleias line the wide grassy banks. There are many flies, maybe they are they sedge flies or maybe they are clegg flies, but I think they are biting me.

After passing Clifton Cruisers, by bridge 66, a large boat coming at full speed careers into me with a glancing blow into the bow – biff! Luckily it has not done any serious damage. Through a small tunnel, I have a small brandy to calm my nerves, then through bridge 42 and out into the countryside.

At 12:45am, I moor past bridge 35, at Hungerfield Oak Wood, and by the hire boats of Rose Narrowboats. There is something I don't like about the place, in a cutting with something unfriendly about the location; I can't put my finger in it. I carry on, with the intention of mooring at 'Ansty'.

As I approach the village, a graffiti skull on a bridge proclaims 'Welcome to Ansty'. There doesn't seem to be any convenient mooring spaces, and the other boats don't look particularly friendly. Ansty is an anagram of Nasty…. I decide to carry on.

Graffiti on the bridge just before Ansty

It is getting late, and there are power lines and roads spoiling the peace. I carry on past the electricity distribution centre, and finally moor in a far more pleasant spot near Hawkesbury junction.

Three horses munch the grass on a clearing by the towpath. The junction is between the end of the Oxford canal and the Coventry Canal. I walk south along the Coventry to get some provisions then back to Moonstone to bake an improvised roast chicken dish with courgettes, potatoes, beetroot, with a salad of fennel, tomatoes, and spring onions. It is very tasty.

Day 13, Wednesday the 9th of July.

It is a breezy, cloudy day with some sunshine. I am off at 8:15am. It takes eight minutes to go through the almost level lock. This lock marks the end of the Oxford Canal, and its junction with the Coventry canal. The many canals around Birmingham were owned by different companies, and they put locks in at the junctions to stop one company saving on pumping costs by 'stealing' the water from the other.

I take the exit onto the Coventry canal and turn right towards Atherstone. Rose, hawthorn, and ash line the canalised river. I pass a boat coming the other way, and a water rat swims over the mirror like surface. The river makes a sharp right hand turn by Bedworth Hill bridge.

By 9am I am in the outskirts of Bedworth with well kept houses adorning PV clad roofs. I pass the entrance to the Ashby canal at 9:25am. The north Birmingham industrialised landscape, with spiked fans protecting pipe bridges, gives way to open countryside with fields of wheat and sweetcorn.

Nearing Nuneaton, I am heading again into suburbia. I pass what I think are Nepalese women walking along the towpath, they giggle in appreciation as I say 'Namesti' ('hello' in Nepalese). I moor by a bridge leading to the town centre at 10:15am. It is market day, the long walk pains my ankle, but the journey is compensated by finding a very good fish stall, and a very large and well stocked Asda supermarket.

Back to the boat, and after a lunchtime snack I set off at 12:55am. There are boatyards and allotments. A strange turf pyramid looms on the horizon. I fill up with water at a countryside marina. I finally moor at 3:05 pm, just before bridge 34 in the countryside, out on a hillside. My dinner consists of scallops potatoes, peas, and beans, and crab. Because of the incessant noise from the farmer's son racing his motorbike around a route which every five minutes reaches the very nearby bridge, I am forced to move on two bridges further up.

Day 14, Thursday the 10th of July

A strange dream, something about a dream number, which in my waking moments I write down as 9609625, which according to numbersaplenty.com is 5^3 x 59 x 1303.

Setting off at 6:43am, it is 18°C and Sunny, with an almost perfectly clear sky.
I pass a grassy spoil tip from the old mining activities. Horses are sunning themselves amongst the reddish tops of the ripening grasses.

Past bridge 38 I reach the outskirts of Atherstone, then by bridges 39 and 40 I am in its heart. There is a strange disagreement about where the TV aerials point, north-east or north-west.

I pass 1950's style brick warehouses, derelict, with broken windows, then at 7:10am I reach the first two locks of a flight of 11 downhill locks..

Out of lock:
                      2@7:43am
                      4@8:11am
                      5@8:23am
                      6@8:43am
                      11@10:07am

After these I am released into open fields of potatoes and spinach then poppies. One white goose is leading ten young white geese. Pairs of ducks are performing some sort of mating ritual with synchronised diving and rhythmic neck movements.

I stop at Polesworth at 11:15am, past bridge 54. There is a good greengrocers. I have a half in the Bulls Head then head back. A little wine, cheese and garlic is very good in the sunshine. Off again at 12:28am.

Oak, ash, and sycamore trees overhang the muddy water, and soon I pass under the motorway bridge. The graffiti hails "Support structures – wives and mothers". An old pit top wheel and pit prop now form a canalside sculpture.

Oak flanked silver birches, then an even more eclectic mix of species. By Alvecote a golf course, we are slowly entering Tamworth. I am out of two locks at 1:55pm. Past Fazely Junction, with skew road bridge signs, and browned out graffiti. I exit Tamworth at 2:55pm. Swifts dart around the trees. I moor just past Hopwas at 3:38pm.

Day 15, Friday the 11th of July

I set off at 8:57am to a somewhat overcast day. On the far bank there is a blockhouse and warning signs that this is an army firing range, it hasn't stopped the locals as using it as an improvised rave site. The previous night amplifiers were being wheeled up the towpath.

The canal seems to be going uphill, an impossibility I know, but I am sure many would agree that it doesn't always appear level, sometimes up sometimes down! This, I suspect, is something to do with a false perspective, created by bankside trees or hedges of different sizes. Behind the reed lined bank, there are modern farm buildings.

At Whittington there is a well-appointed eco-build house, whilst by bridge 78 there are many gnomes amongst the neat gardens. I stop for a break at 10am, walk to the local Co-Op, then off again at 10:51am past foxgloves and honeysuckle and myriads of lilac flowered potatoes.
Between bridges 84 and 85 there is a nice rural stretch then past marinas and a road. By bridge 88 would be a good mooring, but it is too early. Cider drinkers shout "what's your engine"? Reaching the end of the Coventry canal, I arrive at Fradley junction at 12:39am.

Fradley Junction, the Coventry Canal enters from the left

I moor just before the junction, and have some lunch at the 'Mucky Duck' opposite. After lunch I turn left onto the Trent and Mersey canal.

The locks now head uphill. I am out of the first two by 2:40pm. I chat to a relaxed lady who says she has been on the canal for forty years. At the next of these single width locks I forget the dangers of not having your boat right up at the front. Even with a small gap of a foot or so between the bow of your boat and the top gate, and half way through the filling process, the boat gets pushed back, then leaps forward like a bucking bronco, and surges forward at speed into the gate. The crash causes many items to fall off shelves inside. This time, luckily, it wasn't too severe, the Worcestershire sauce bottle being the only casualty.

I moor at 4:05pm in a wood, but soon it is apparent that there is a biting midge problem, so reluctantly I set off again. Through Rugely, past the cooling towers of the power station, I wonder why these ugly industrial monuments were accepted.

The power station near Rugely

I pass through the town, and just past the aqueduct I moor at 6:55pm. On retrospect, I should have moored in town by bridge 66. I check the fuel on the bamboo stick, it is down to 13.0 cm. After some food, I enjoy trying to do a watercolour sketch of a striking full moon, maybe it's a super-moon.

Day 16, Saturday the 12th of July.

It is sunny, but there is high cloud gathering and I am off at 10:28am. I notice that a bypass has spoilt the view from the canal. A sign on bridge 67 says it was built in 2007.

I pass well to do houses at little Heyford, to catch up with other boats, as there is a queue for the lock. I am relaxed and in no hurry. Nearby there are the sounds of a shoot. Finally I get through the lock by bridge 71 at 12:33am. I moor and walk to a ridiculously expensive local shop whose prices reflect the self-image of the people here. The surprise disappears as I reach the next lock and I see on the map that we are entering the grounds of Shugborough House.

Shugborough House

The house and grounds, now bequeathed to the National Trust, was the home of the Earl of Litchfield. The last Earl of Litchfield was more famous as the photographer Patrick Litchfield. An earlier Earl of Litchfield was Lord Admiral Anson, around the time of Nelson

To reach the house from the canal I walk across a beautiful stone pedestrian bridge over the river Trent, where families and children are picnicking and playing joyfully in the shallow waving water weeded trout stream. I go round Patrick Litchfield's former home with its ornate dining room, sumptuous lounge, and Chinese summerhouse.

Back to the boat, and a beautiful pristine sixty five foot narrowboat has moored behind. The owners are happy when I compliment them of such a well kept home.

Moored just below Shugborough lock near the house

Now is a decision point. I could reach Chester by continuing up the Trent and Mersey canal, but this involves going through a rather long tunnel in which there has recently been an accident, so instead I will go past Stafford to the start of the Shropshire Union canal near Wolverhampton.

I go through the small lock by Shugburough, then a short distance to the Great Heywood junction, taking the Staffordshire and Worcestershire canal to the left, back around the rear of the Shugborough Estate and into a big lake – the Tixall Wide. It is overlooked by a strange and rather ominous old building resembling a gatehouse, known as the Tixall Obelisk. I am now well around the north of Birmingham, and heading south towards the start of the Shropshire Union canal which heads north again up to Chester. To the south east is Cannock Chase forest.

At 4pm I moor at the end of a long line of boats enjoying the view over the lake. The weather is slowly deteriorating to rain. I cook myself a piece of salmon, grilled, with lemon and salad.

As I scan the TV channels I find a repeat of the political drama 'House of cards'. A tale of how a cold and steely civil servant, Francis Irquart with a like minded ruthless wife, gets involved with political intrigue and eventually murder, as he follows his ambition to become prime minister. Never having paid much attention to the series when it was first aired, I become intrigued by the clever insight into ruthless politics. I stay awake for three hour long episodes, but am too tired to watch the last and final one.

Day 17, Sunday the 13<u>th</u> of July

Half of a delicious Craster Kipper on toast does wonders for my waking body. I set off at 8:20am, then through Tixall lock at 8:45am. It is grey and threatens to drizzle as I navigate the windy course of the canal through the wide flat flood plain.

This is the land of the potteries. Passing through pine forests, the canal then takes a turn to the left on an aqueduct over the river Sow valley. At 10am I moor up at bridge 99 with the intention of exploring and stocking up on food. I am on the outskirts of Baswich on the left, with the river Penk and Stafford on the right, Reaching the centre of Stafford by bus, I note an impressive town square, and some remnants of the old medieval curved streets, though much is a mishmash of haphazard development.

A quaint side street in Stafford

Back to the boat, I set off again at 1:28pm. Away from Baswich, through the first lock, the vista opens up onto wide cornfields, then into the edge of Acton Trussell with its modest new build houses with beautifully kept flower gardens. Finally I get to Penkridge, a peaceful family village, and moor between the two town locks at 4pm. I make a delicious paella for supper.

Day 18, Monday 14th July

I start at 8:40am. It is difficult to moor by the second town lock, and there is a queue of hire boats waiting to get through. I finally clear this lock at 9:15am.

A short distance away, at 9:30am I notice a marina at Atherton, and decide to fill up with diesel. It seems I have the last few litres from their tank, and luckily no sign of sludge. A careful calculation indicates that 1cm on my stick gauge is equal to 1.5 gallons, just about the amount on average I have been using per day.

I get away at 9:50am, and am under the A5 – the Roman Watling Street – then through 'Gailey' lock, the fifth of the day at 11:25am. I finally stop for a break and a cheese sandwich, then under the M54 at 1:55pm.

A trench hacked into the rock under 'Gravelly Way' bridge no 78 marks what was originally a tunnel. This was the canal building style here, hacking through rock with dynamite and pick axes, and using the spoil to build aqueducts. The very ancient canal here winds around the surrounding hilly terrain.

Reaching the outskirts of Wolverhampton the wide canal is lined by rows of poplar trees on the left, and a park on the right. The van of an enterprising business offering to wash wheelie bins!

I reach the start of the Shropshire Union Canal at Autherly junction. There is a chaotic queue for the very shallow entry lock.

Long traditional boats are turning and manoeuvring right across the Worcestershire canal by the entrance. Finally it is my turn to enter the Shropshire Union canal, and with welcome help I am under the entry bridge, through the shallow lock, and topping up with water by 2:33pm.

To the left: The entrance to the Shropshire Union canal

Soon the canal is into open countryside. Myriads of Swifts flit from the waterside bushes disturbed by the noise of Moonstone. After the rural setting I pass through 'Park Gate' bridge no 8, into a deep tree lined cutting, and under tall arch of bridge 10, through Braewood to moor at 5:23pm, just past the cutting.

I cook a lamb and vegetable curry with rice which tastes very good.

Day 19, Tuesday the 15th of July

Off at 8:15am, and heading north, at 8:30am I cross again the East-West aligned A5 road, built over the ancient Roman Watling Street, this time looking down over the passing cars from an aqueduct.

I pass a turquoise breasted kingfisher, a rare occasion, as they normally fly away in a shimmer of colour before the boat gets near. The canal passes over a long aqueduct, which would be perfect for mooring with a wide view over the adjoining countryside, except that a hidden underwater ledge would bang on the hull even whilst ten inches from the bank.

Through a lock at 9:05am, then I stop at pleasant Wheaton Aston with its very good shops. I leave at 10:15am and am through Cowley tunnel at 11:53am, to moor for lunch at midday. Feeling sleepy, I make my way to the 'Boat', an old and traditional inn overlooking the canal, where a beautiful barmaid serves me with a half pint of beer and a delicious chicken liver pâté and toast. I pass through Gnosall, then, at 4:11pm moor on another aqueduct between bridges 50 and 51.

View from the aqueduct just past Gnosall

Day 20, Wednesday the 16th of July

A sunny day, and after a half of a Craster kipper on toast, I set off at 7:23am.
There is a nice view of the cornfields to the south west I reach bridge 57 at 8:08am.
Then I pass into the deep rock faced Woodseaves cutting.

Originally the twenty seven mile long section of the Shropshire Union canal from Autherley junction to Nantwich was called the Birmingham and Liverpool junction canal, and was built by Thomas Telford's company between 1825 and 1835. Telford was the first to use cast iron for bridges and aqueducts. They built this canal with pick axes at an average rate of twelve metres per day.

'Jurassic Park' near Market Drayton

In this Jurassic Park jungle setting I reach a flight of five locks at 8:45am, and clear them by 9:43am, then to moor at Market Drayton at 10am.

As I walk into town. There is a sense of poverty, poor health and aggravation. In the market at the centre, I buy a pristine large antique wooden handled screwdriver, just right to disassemble the hand drawn claxon on the boats roof, that is almost completely jammed, and in need of a good service.

Back to the boat and off at 11:30am. It is twelve miles to Nantwich. I reach the six locks at Adderly at 12:35 pm. Coming the other way is a team dressed as Victorians with red cravats and flat cloth caps. They are from a 'living steam museum' in Ellesmere Port at the top end of the canal, and are working their way up the locks with the steam powered boat 'President'. Their boat consumes two large bags of coal for a day's travel, compare that to my small economical 1950's diesel that uses just six litres.

Finally I am out of this lock flight at 1:58pm, only to reach the Audlem flight of fifteen locks at 2:15pm. I get through the first eight in just one hour – a speed record, but helped by the boats coming the other way, who leave each following lock filled and ready with its top gate open.

I moor after lock 13 at 4:46pm. The village, with its crane and wharf side warehouse, was obviously an important staging post. Quite a few people are gathered outside the 'Shropshire Fly'. I have two pints and an enjoyable evening chatting to the local and very varied canal folk.

Day 21, Thursday the 17th July

Off at 8am and through the two remaining Audlem flight locks by 8:30am. Above an almost clear blue sky with a little bit of cirrus promises a fine day. Out into lovely countryside, but spoiled on the left by a huge new marina. To my estimate it houses over two hundred boats.

A sign advertises trips around Hack Green, a local cold war secret nuclear bunker. I walk the few hundred yards, but at

9:15am it is too early to go around. I am actually glad not to be reminded of the madness and horrors of planning for the possible apocalypse of that period.

A country cottage near the nuclear bunker

I get through the nearby pair of locks by about 10:45am. Soon afterwards I reach Nantwich and find a local boatyard where replace an empty gas canister. I decide to moor, but after failing to find a suitable mooring space just beyond the town, I turn around and moor on the town aquaduct twenty foot above the ring road.

It seems the perfect place to leave the boat and head home for a few days. I proceed to locate the train station for a return trip back to. Near the station is a pub full of Beatles memorabilia. After a short fifteen minute hop on a single carriage train to Crewe, I take a super speedy Virgin 'Pendolino' train back into London Euston. The population contrast is stark; it really brings to my attention just how many people there are per square mile in London. Finally back home I deal with mail, email, washing and watering.

Day 22, Friday the 18th of July

I do more household chores; attend to an order for some research equipment from the National Physical Laboratory no less. I mow the lawn; get a bit of sun in my small suburban garden. I am so so tired, so tired…….I sleep quite well in spite of the heat.

Day 23, Saturday the 19th of July

There is nothing more to do at home, I make an on the spur decision to return to the boat.

Setting out at midday, and I am lucky with the trains, but at Crewe there is no connection for the short hop to Nantwich for over forty minutes. I decide to locate the bus stop, which is a fair walk away. A bus finally arrives, and after a long drive through congested roads with a grey sky and a bit of drizzle, I end up in an unfamiliar part of Nantwich, and proceed to walk in the wrong direction.

When I finally get back to the boat it is nearly 5pm, there is an ominous smell as I enter. The fridge has been off – I failed to re-light it when I changed the gas bottle, and most of my food has gone off in the heat. I have to clean the fridge right out, and then, exhausted, reluctantly walk back into town to re-stock from Morrisons.

On the way I spy two Indian restaurants next to each other, displaying their 'food hygiene score' in the window. I decide to try the one with full marks!

Returning to the boat with my supplies and meal I can at last relax. The curry was delicious, and I can report now, did my digestive system only good.

Day 24, Sunday the 20th of July

Up at 7:30am. I go for a walk, with the idea of getting more supplies, but I have forgotten that it is Sunday. There are no shops for bread or beer or anything until 11am.

At 8:30am I start the engine and set off, but I am facing the wrong direction. In spite of the relatively short length of my boat – 36ft – I am just unable to turn around in the width of the 'aqueduct' style canal, my judgement hasn't allowed for the submerged step next to the edge.
I have seen boats with small go-kart tyres, horizontal in the water as bankside fenders. Their significance dawns on me. With such improvised wide fenders, you CAN moor almost anywhere on the high up aqueduct sections of this canal, with peace of mind, and without an incessant 'knock-knock' on the hull.

In order to turn around, I have to go half a mile or so, right to the outskirts, and then proceed back through the town, heading again north towards Chester.

I am finally out of Nantwich at 10am, past Henhull moorings as the canal widens.
I pass the entry to the Llangollan canal at 10:25am – famous for its high aqueduct. It would be good to experience this canal, but it would add at least a week to my journey, and I am not tempted to enter another flight of locks, especially when it is the height of the holiday season, and is likely to be full of hire boats.

I pass the junction with the Middlewich canal at 10:55am which links the Shropshire Union canal with the Trent and Mersey canal. I keep straight on towards Chester and reach the Bunbury pair of staircase locks at 12:13pm.

In a staircase lock, the exit gate of one lock is the entry gate for the next lock. This does speed the lock process, but requires that all locks in the staircase are in the correct state: full or empty, before entering the flight. In this case of descending a pair of locks the top lock needs to be full, and the bottom one empty. Emptying the top lock then fills the lower lock.

I have paired up with another boat through this 'flight'. The couple on it are charming and friendly. Shortly after this staircase we get to Beeston, where there are two famous locks, first the 'Stone lock' followed by the 'Iron lock'.

I am advised that although double width, the Iron lock should be treated with caution, as it is possible for boats to jam as the water is lowered. I heed the caution and let the other boat through first. When they are through and the lock refilled, I bring Moonstone in and close the top gates. I hold the boat from a centre line from the side of the lock, my preferred way, as it avoids climbing up or down ladders into the lock.

Once Iron lock is empty, I realise I have a problem. A foot bridge spans the lock just below the bottom gates, and I cannot swing the rope underneath this. I have done this manoeuvre several times in the past, but it requires a boat hook to catch the dangling rope, and I have left mine on the boat, which is now inaccessible being below in the empty lock with no ladder. I signal to a boat waiting to come up that I would like to borrow their boat hook. They kindly acknowledge this, and armed with this implement, it is a matter of seconds for me to loop the rope under the bridge, and pull Moonstone out of the lock.

I catch up with the couple in the boat I came down the Bunbury staircase with. I join them in the 'Shade Oak' for a pint and a well endowed prawn sandwich. He is a street lighting designer by trade, but really wants to be a self employed horologist. They obviously both enjoy being on the canal. It is 4pm already, I carry on and finally moor at 6:25pm between bridges 116 and 117, out in the countryside with a view of a local village church spire over a field of sweet corn. The village is Waverton, just five miles from Chester. The phone and TV reception are very marginal.

The village of Waverton from the canal

Day 25, Monday the 21st of July

I enjoy fried egg, shitaki mushroom, chorizo and tomatoes on toast for breakfast, and set off at 7:55am to a clear blue sky.

At Waverton neat canal side bungalows look down to the canal and I am through 'Egg' Bridge at 8:12am.

I reach the first lock of the day and pair up with a seventy-foot hire boat packed with eight related Australians. It seems many English speaking families from the outreaches of what was the British Empire are nowadays lured back here for canal boat based family reunions. We are out of this lock at 8:56am, then a second lock by 9:10am, then a flight of three, out of number two at 9:53am. The old industrial heart of Chester is coming into view with a huge water tower and other reconditioned industrial buildings.

The Shropshire Union canal through Chester

There is nowhere to moor on the long stretch through the town so I continue around the steep sandstone Roman city wall and to the remaining staircase flight of three, the steepest in the country, down to a more tranquil basin by the spur canal to the river Dee, still near to Chester town centre and moor at 11:15am.

Chester staircase locks

The basin by the spur canal to the river Dee

It soon becomes apparent that this is not the most ideal mooring spot as it is by a bench habituated by a professional beggar and tramp. His continuous effort to expunge guilt and money from passers by makes me feel uncomfortable. I visit the town for supplies, in the hope that he will not be there when I return, but unfortunately he is still there.

The medieval centre of Chester, rebuilt by the Victorians

I return to the medieval museum of a town centre to look around. I walk through the cathedral, the town hall, and finally go on a tour bus around the city. This is a good experience except that the ageing tour guide commentary is filled mostly with his chirpy cheeky wit which doesn't work on me, and leaves me feeling a little disappointed by the tour.

I return back to the boat at 4:30pm, there is no tramp to be seen. I start my dinner in peace. Unfortunately he returns again, so I do make the effort to chat to him. He claims that he was in the army in Northern Ireland and saw his friend shot in the head. He has been a professional beggar in Chester for the last forty years since then, but he would go back 'like a shot' into the army to kill in Iraq, if they would have him.

I decide to take the earliest opportunity to move on, anxious not to raise any vexation, and for a peaceful night free from concerns about mad axmen. I head two and a half miles out of town towards Ellesmere Port, and finally find a peaceful spot in parkland, mooring at 7:09pm. I finish my dinner as it gets dark. It is a very clear night and I take some photos of the starry sky banded by the Milky Way.

Day 26, Tuesday the 22nd of July

Well that's it! Time to turn around, the few miles to Ellesmere Port at the end of the canal doesn't look that interesting.

After Peshwari Nan, saved from the Nantwich take away, with bacon and mushroom for breakfast, I set off at 9:05am, turn around, and shortly reach again the basin below the three staircase locks. There is a queue for the locks, so I decide to do some shopping. I find some quality food in a small Waitrose over the far side of town.

Back to the boat, and another boat is heading to the locks – I ask if I can ascend the flight with them. Even though my ankle is badly swollen, I climb the internal ladder my side to work the gates. There are some helpers on this side from a boat above the flight waiting to come down, so I don't climb up at the middle lock.

In spite of my efforts I am scolded – I feel quite unfairly - by both of the middle aged couple on the other boat for not sharing the workload. Finally we are out of this flight at 11:31am. I am back through Chester away from Mr and Mrs Grumpy, and up out of locks 5 and 6 by 12:40am.

I pass through lock 7 with a very pleasant couple at 1:06pm. I am up through lock 9 by 1:55 and stop at the 'Cheshire Cat' for a lunchtime pint. Then I travel back through Christleton and Waverton, and past the long stretch of farmland moorings.

I moor just past the Spade Oak pub at Bates Mill Bridge, 108, at about 5pm. A tasty meal of venison, potato and cabbage is washed down with some good Shiraz.

Day 27, Wednesday the 23rd of July

After bacon, egg and 'ear' mushrooms, I set off at 7:55am. I open the nearby lock, pair up with another boat, then out at 8:28am. Sparkling bubbles appear and pop on the still sunlit surface. This is a beautiful stretch: small hills and oak trees on the left, and a crack willow lined tow path on the right. Further on on the right, is a railway, old mine workings, spoil tips and the Beeston signal box on stilts.

Through the iron lined iron lock at 9:05am, then through stone lock by 9:20am. With the bright sun dancing on the water I am gliding through a gently curved wooded stretch.

Then through the last lock before the twin staircase at 9:48am, then through the pair by 10:48am.
I pass narrowboat 'Rondinella' with its beautiful hand painted design of swallows swifts or martins flitting around the sky.

I am past the Middlewich junction at 11:36am. The first canal here ran from Ellesmere port to Chester, on to Nantwich in 1779, but the link from the Middlewich junction across to the Trent and Mersey canal wasn't completed until 1833.
I am back past the Llangollan junction at 12:05pm.

I stop at Nantwich at 12:42pm, and get 60 litres of diesel. Adding this brings the stick measure from 13.0cm to 21.3cm, so according to this addition, a centimetre represents 7.2 litres or 1.72 gallons. Over the last two days I have only consumed 1.55 gallons, so a correct assumption for Moonstone is indeed about a gallon a day.

I stock up at Morrisons, then leave at about 2:30pm. Out of Hack Green lock 1 at 3:15pm then up through Hack Green lock 2 at 3:30pm and past the nuclear bunker.

After passing the large new marina, I reach Audlem, below the lock flight, and moor at 5:30pm.
Here boats are amassing for a festival and vintage car rally over the weekend. I recognise a classic boat called 'Elizabeth' that used to be at Cassiobury Lock near Watford.

Over sixty foot long, with a double row of square windows, Elizabeth, an ocean liner fantasy. was a horse drawn coke carrying boat until 1928, then towed on the Trent until 1935. It has had various engines since then. Its current owner – since 1966 - has moved up to Middlewich.

Everyone is very friendly and chatty. It seems that many boats are from Middlewich, and that it is a haven for many who live full time on their boats. I return to Moonstone, have some food, then walk up to the 'Shropshire Fly', where the young staff are having a business meeting with the owner. I have a conversation with a sprightly extrovert lady whose husband, introverted and dour, is the complete opposite. Having drunk too much I actually feel quite sober, leaving for the stroll back to the boat in the dark at 12:30pm.

Day 28, Thursday the 24th of June

I set off at 8:10am to face the 15 uphill locks of the Audlem flight. I get the boat into the first lock. As I am about to close the gates there is a cry 'room for one more?'. Indeed there is. Although these are single width locks, Moonstone is 34', whilst this boat is probably about 30', so we can pack into the 74' lock.

I am a bit concerned about the appearance of the owner – a long chin bearded, tattooed, hell's angel with dog, however, his professional approach to sharing the work on the lock gates and sluices soon puts my mind at rest.

His name is Martin and his boat, a sturdy live aboard, is called 'Rascal'. By the time we are in the third lock, he is on his phone, and says he has arranged for some help from a British Waterways man. This is a reference to two of his friends Colin and Carol who live on a trad boat up this way at Middlewich, and who are staying at the historic boat festival this weekend.

They arrive and we speed up the flight like a supersonic aeroplane, exiting the fifteen lock flight by 10:15am. That is 2hr 5mins for 15 locks, an average of 8 minutes a lock! We thank and say farewell to Colin and Carol, then on to a shorter flight of six locks, the ones through 'Jurassic Park', these done by 11:30am.

We both stop at Market Drayton where I go to buy wine, water, and a Lotto ticket for Judith, who has emailed me from a holiday in Canada, with a request to buy a specific set of numbers for her home bound old uncle. This is tricky. What if I get the wrong numbers and his came up and won? I am very careful to get the correct ticket, and put it in a safe memorable place on the boat.

Off again with 'Rascal' at 2:30pm, reaching another flight of five locks at 3pm. Out of these at 3:45pm then I am going through the deep sunlit jungle cutting with its tall viaduct bridge. I finally moor opposite the Wharf Tavern at Goldstone at 4:30pm. Twenty seven locks today!

The Wharf Tavern at Goldstone

At dusk, a speedy new 60' boat, which I believe I remember from earlier in the day, arrives and moors by the bridge.

Day 29, Friday the 25th of July

Off at 8:30am. Swifts, or are they Martins, congregate in the hawthorn hedges. I pass bridge 50 where I moored over a week ago, with its views of fields and a distant hilly ridge.

Under bridge 41 at 10:36am and into the 'Grub Street' cutting, gloriously green from the high angled sunshine. Through the Telegraph bridge 39, with its telegraph pole top perched on a special middle arch. I reach Norbury junction where the disused Newport branch used to run at 11:12am, then the Shelbury aqueduct and Gnosall at 11:53am.

I stop for lunch at the Navigation pub at 12:06pm and start again at 1:45pm. By bridge 19 at Wheaton Aston there is a really old fashioned garage with old petrol pumps and a canalside service offering the cheapest diesel in the region, at the moment running at just 70.9 pence per litre – too late to take advantage of these prices, I paid 86p/lr when I topped up at Nantwich.

At 3:46pm I have passed through the last but one one remaining lock of this lower section of the Shropshire canal. The weather looks changeable; there are thunderclouds in the sky. The canal passes over the A5 again; the old Roman road, Watling Street.

I pass Martin and 'Rascal' who have moored for the day. He says he has decided to go back to London around the North of Birmingham – fewer locks. I am going around the south, despite ninety one locks, having come this far I don't want to retrace my steps.

I moor just south of Braewood, out of the cutting, at 5:45pm. I ponder the decision about my route, after Birmingham, this will involve the Hatton flight of twenty one locks downhill, followed by a flight of another twenty one afterwards, and some more: a total of ninety one locks I am told.

A psychedelic mushroom bedecked shark boat!

That night I have a strange dream about going up a flight of locks where each lock required a small cylinder on the lock gate to be filled from a bottle of water before it would work.

Day 30, Saturday the 26th of July

Off at 7:03am.

An improvised workshop under the shelter of a convenient bridge

I reach the anti water theft lock at Autherly junction at 8:22am, then turn right and down the Staffs and Worcester canal for a short hop.

Here are the old borderlands of Birmingham. Massive railway arches, pipes and bridges feed the old industrial centre. I take a left turn towards the start of the twenty one lock Wolverhampton flight, moor, and discover the meaning of last nights dream: the locks require special keys to be inserted into small metal cylinders. I have no such key. Before any panic sets in, a respectable looking sixty foot boat 'Straight and Narrow' turns into the cut, and to my amazement and gratitude lends me the magic implement.

I am offered the lead, and soon we are followed by a third boat. We all help one another, and it is warming to feel that the ascent of this mad twenty one lock flight is a goal shared by us all.

For those of an 'anorak' or 'train spotting' disposition, here is a table of the times for the locks

Lock count	Lock no	Time out	Time for lock
1	21(in)	8:50 am	
1	21	8:58 am	13 min
2	20	9:11 am	13 min
3	19	9:24 am	14 min
4	18	9:38 am	15 min
5	17	9:53 am	16 min
6	16	10:09 am	14 min
7	15	10:23 am	11 min
8	14	10:34 am	9 min
9	13	10:43 am	13 min
10	12	10:56 am	13 min
11	11	11:07 am	12 min
12	10	11:20 am	12 min
13	9	11:33 am	13 min
14	8	11:44 am	11 min
15	7	11:55 am	11 min
16	6	12:04 am	9 min
17	5	12:14 am	10 min
18	4	12:25 am	11 min
19	3	12:35 am	10 min
20	2	12:46 am	11 min
21	1	12:58am	12 min

About a third of the way up, and the exercise and achievement is making me giddy, like a whirling dervish. Two thirds of the way up and I meet the first of the days boats coming down the lock flight. This is encouraging since it means that the remaining locks should all be ready and empty. As the lock gates open, opened by a grey haired lady, they reveal a very pretty flower painted boat with a rather stern looking man with a handlebar moustache. Somehow he reminds me of one of those old Prussian soldiers, I can imagine a pointed brass hat on his head. I move the boat to the left by the towpath. To my amazement he heads directly towards me. I am at a standstill, and as I see him continue to approach, apparently blind to my presence, I go into full reverse. Even though I am reversing furiously, he hits my boat almost head on, gouging the paintwork of my bow insignia. To add insult to injury he shouts at me telling me it is my fault!

As our three boats reach the top of the flight at about 1pm, we give ourselves a final gasp of self congratulation

View from above the top lock of the Wolverhampton flight

We all stop for a short break just past the top lock, and then set off to Tipton at 1:18pm. The water is beautifully clear, but very soon turns jet black, whether this is because of the need for dredging, or the remnants of coal dust from the industrial revolution is unclear, but the prop and engine seem to be overworking as black smoke emits from the exhaust, It is rather worrying, and I am relieved to see that it isn't just my old Lister engine that is having trouble, clouds of smoke are coming from the boats in front. It is just hard work as a result of some sort of canal weed that is like tangled fishing line, and almost as strong. I plough on.

The start of the fishing line weed of industrialised Wolverhampton

Black water turns coppery blue green as we pass ageing industrial sites. A sign says Birmingham ten miles and three locks. That sounds encouraging. By 2:40pm we reach a tunnel which is short but very wet.

Disturbing the lockside fishermen at 3pm, we reach Tipton, the start of a short downhill flight, and are out of the three locks by 3:45pm.

I have a chance to talk to the others. Colin and Anne are in 'Straight and Narrow' followed by 'Harold' then followed like the tortoise following the hares, by 'Moonstone'!.

The Birmingham 'main line' canal is long and straight, and high above the roads below.

By 4:46pm we have reached Bromfield Junction where a parallel canal is accessible through a three lock rise and fall. Keeping on the level section we reach Gas Street Basin where I find a mooring space at 6:13pm. The boat moored behind is 'Obsession' owned by Steve and Audrey who are friendly and welcoming. I walk back to Colin and Anne on 'Straight and Narrow' and return the special lock key with my thanks.

The centre of Birmingham has been totally regenerated, and feels very comfortable and safe. Gas Street Basin itself has many waterside bars and restaurants packed full of tourists. It is bedecked with flowers.

Day 31, Sunday the 27th of July

I decide to stay put for a while, and explore the centre of Birmingham on foot.
I walk along the old locks which I have been told is not the best route on a boat, and finally find the Waitrose 'Mecca'.

Walking back past the cathedral, through the central plaza near New Street station, a Hari Chrisna group has stalls and a large stunning decorated elephant sculpture.

Another walk takes me to a chandler by some private moorings where I buy a special lock key for myself. I look around the IKON gallery – I seem to remember being involved in a video art event here way back in the late seventies. Then I go around a huge cubical building that turns out to be the theatre and library. From its roof there is a wonderful view, and I can just see Moonstone between the buildings.

Gas Street Basin

Although interesting, I have that urge to move on. I set off at 3:50pm, and travel out through Gas Street Basin, the canal turning right and heading towards Edgebaston. This way out avoids the immediate lock flight.

I moor at Edgebaston, near the university at 4:30pm. Its not quite satisfactory – trip boats keep passing and causing the boat to bang on the stones of the bank, and then later some music festival starts up the other side of the commuter railway line. I decide to try and reach it rather than suffer, but it proves to be too far a walk. At 7:45pm I set off once more, and at 8:45pm I moor quite close to Bournville railway station, painted in the colours of Cadbury's chocolate wrappers, to eat a tasty grilled chicken dinner.

Day 32, Monday the 28th of July

It is a bright and sunny morning; I set off at 8:30am. Immediately a shopping bag fouls the prop, but with much reversing, it is finally released. I pass the violet Cadbury station with its Magritte like morning commuters waiting patiently on the platform, and reach Kings Norton junction at 9am. Here I am turning left off the Staffordshire and Worcester canal onto the Stratford on Avon canal with its first Guillotine lock.

The Guillotine lock at the start of the Stratford on Avon canal

A pedestrian sadly tells me that I will soon encounter a dead swan. Indeed there is, spattered with blood, and another, alive but worse for wear. I am told that it could be an attack by vandals rather than foxes. The living injured swan is silent and shocked,

Passing through Brandwood tunnel at 9:22am I reach a long peaceful wooded glade and 'Lyons boatyard'. After more suburbia, then I reach Shirley drawbridge at 10:27am, clearing this at 10:41am. Then back in the countryside, followed by an unlikely isolated development of many flats in the middle of open fields with sheep. On reaching Great Haywood, there is a strong smell of cinnamon.

I reach bridge 18 at 11:46am then Warings Green wharf by bridge 22 at 12:14pm. Followed by 'boundary' bridge 23 at 12:22pm, and Hockley Heath drawbridge at 12:57pm. This is followed by yet another drawbridge which I am out of at 1:15pm then a long downhill lock flight:

Lock no	Time out	Time (mins)
1	1:10 (in)	
1	1:25	15e
2	1:37	12e
3	1:45	8
4	2:04	19
5	2:12	8
6	2:26	14
7	2:33	7
8	2:44	11
9	2:56	12
10	3:01	5
11	3:07	6
12	3:16	9
13	3:26	10
14	3:36	10
15	3:46	10
16	3:55	9
17	4:07	12
18	4:13	6
19	4:25	12
20	4:38	13

3hr 28mins for 20 locks.

At the bottom, I take a short junction section at Kingswood Brook and then I am back on the Grand Union canal heading south. I moor at Rowington, near 'Tom O'the Wood' at 5:01pm. I cook a tasty lamb spaghetti bolognaise.

Day 33, Tuesday the 29th of July

I set off at 9:05am. It is a sunny day, the canal winds slowly on a hillside overlooking the village of Rowington. Then I reach Shrewley tunnel, with its extra side tunnel for the barge horses to walk through. The main tunnel is wet and misty, with ducks playing just in from its far exit. I am out at about10am.

Shrewley tunnel

By 11am I have reached the top and start of the Hatton lock flight. These are big double locks, with heavy double gates both in and out. .

There are twenty two of these in short succession. The paddle winding gear is manually operated hydraulic, and the whole gate paddle winding system set in a slightly off- vertical cylinder, with a white painted top with a protruding rod gives the appearance of a giant candle with its wick. Each lock had four candles – or fork handles if you are familiar with the two Ronnie's sketch.

The whole flight of locks gives a surrealist appearance of a Roman Catholic procession. Sharing the locks with another boat, we make good time.

Lock no	Time out	Time
1	11:10 (in)	
1	11:19	9
2	11:21	3
3	11:34	13
4	11:42	8
5	11:48	6
6	11:54	6
7	12:01	7
8	12:-8	7
9	12:14	6
10	12:21	7
11	12:30	9
12	12:39	9
13	12:53	14
14	12:59	6
15	1:07	8
16	1:15	8
17	1:24	9
18	1:32	8
19	1:45	13
20	2:01	13
21	2:09	8
22	2:18	9

Fast indeed! 3h8m total.

View from the top of the Hatton Flight

Not far to go to Warwick. There are noticeably more aeroplanes crossing the sky, presumably from Birmingham.

At 2:39pm I moor up the re-dug Saltisford spur, which is run by an enthusiastic boat community who cajole the visitors boats into the available slots. I get a good space with its own pontoon, by a canalside garden. I check the fuel level, which is now 16.5cm. This means that my average fuel consumption over the last week amounts to just 4.9 litres, or just over a gallon, per day.

Dusk on the Saltisford Spur, Warwick

I walk up to the centre of Warwick, and spy the castle. Walking round to the entrance, I am met with disappointment to discover that it is now run by Legoland, and an adult entry ticket is £24!!! It is getting late, most people are leaving. I follow the crowd, only to find I am in the car park, with no way out except for a long walk, re-tracing my steps.

In the evening I have a delicious venison steak with lemon, potatoes, and broccoli.

Two white geese on this peaceful spur visit the boats in turn for bread.

Day 34, Wednesday the 30th of July

Breakfast then travel back out of the Saltisford spur by 8:57am, then through a pair of locks below Warwick by 9:45am.

Past Kate's cruisers boatyard, then by 10am I am halfway between Warwick and Royal Leamington Spa. The canal passes high above a railway.

Entering the outskirts of town, the modern wharf stylised apartment blocks and waterside lawns give a garden city feel to the canal, despite the looming electricity pylons. By 10:34am, I am near the centre of Royal Leamington Spa, and decide to do some shopping, and maybe explore the town.

I have no great hopes because of the disappointment with Warwick. At least I can see that there's a nearby Co-Op. As I walk towards the centre of town, I feel happier as the architecture starts to remind me of Paris, the iron that cast and curved at the turn of the century.

Royal Leamington Spa

The streets widen out, and I can see that this town was indeed worthy of its 'Spa' status. Council gardeners are working hard on the yellow and violet flowerbeds, and I feel that they should be rightly proud of their work.

I stop at a charity shop to buy the complete works of Lewis Carol for £2. Nearby there is a 'Bong' shop for hippies and new agers. There are so many glorious Victorian stone buildings here: The Town Hall, the Victoria Bank, and the Spa museum and Art Gallery.

The Spa Museum is both interesting and disappointing. To me it is disappointing because the Spa has been shut down. No longer can you bathe in the mysterious mineral waters. No longer can you even drink the spa water.

According to the lady in charge of the museum there is a stone obelisk outside, with taps from which, I am told, you are able to sample the real spa water. I am even provided with a small plastic cup, courtesy of the Spa Museum. But as I go outside into the street to try this, I find that no amount of pushing the button on the tap on the stone plinth produced anything more than a burp and a single drip! I return to the museum, and explain that no water comes out. The lady in charge expresses no concern, just waves me off with "Oh, they must have shut it off because of contamination". No care, just a broad assumption. I walk away in disgust at the way modern bureaucracy has swept aside the pride of the Victorians.

I return to the boat and set off again at 1:17pm. I realise there is a further flight of locks which I should tackle today. I reach the first at 2:15pm, then:

Lock no	Time out	Time (mins)
1	2:15 (in)	
1	2:30	15
2	2:45	15
3	3:00	15
4	3:20	20
5	3:38	18
6	4:11	33
7	4:25	14
8	4:45	20
9	4:50	15
10	5:00	10

It is a long struggle, much of the ascending flight requiring the next lock to be prepared, and most without the help of another boat crew. It feels like climbing a mountain towards a Victorian lock cottage near the top.

I reach Long Itchington, not far from the top of the flight, and moor a few hundred yards past the 'Two Boats' inn, one of the two pubs here. In one of them, a very sexy barmaid is apparently having an affair with the landlord.

I have a half, return to the boat for a fish pie supper, then back to the pub where I have a long chat with an old yokel who built narrowboats all his life.

We disagree strongly about the indiscriminate slaughter in Gaza by the Israelis, which is the current news topic. I am saved in the nick of time, by the call of 'time'.

Day 35, Thursday the 31st of July

I set off at about 9am. Only a short distance to yet another set of locks – the Stockton flight:

Lock no	Time out	Time (mins)
1	9:05(in)	
1	9:21	17
2	9:37	16
3	9:54	17
4	10:04	10
5	10:14	10
6	10:25	11
7	10:37	12

I am followed up the flight by a traditionally painted hotel boat, with four young eager and helpful crew members, in turn looking after eight passengers.

At the top I pass a strange boat name 'Edoba Dexifon', the name is in fact 'No Fixed Abode' spelt backwards.

With reeded banks and open countryside, this stretch is reminiscent of the nearby Oxford canal. I note that strange 'uphill' illusion about this curved section, and also note that the illusion disappears as the canal reaches a straight section. Just three locks remain before the junction:

Lock no	Time out	Time (mins)
1	11:49	
2	12:00	11
3	12:14	14

Arriving at the Napton junction at 12:27pm, and, turning right onto the Oxford Canal, I am finally back on familiar land. This is both welcoming and sad because it is the end of the new territory, which becomes rarer and rarer the longer one has owned a narrowboat.

At 1:10pm I stop at the bottom of the uphill Napton flight to get some supplies from a local shop, since I know the next stretch to be well away from civilisation.

Starting up the flight of ten locks, I make good progress. There is a constant stream of boats coming down, so each lock in turn is ready. I am sorry for those coming down. Halfway up there is a queue, some boats have waited for over an hour for one lock.

Clear of the top lock it is getting overcast and starts to rain heavily. I moor just past bridge 123, near Priors Hardwick, and cook a tasty chicken and courgette curry. Before sunset, the rain stops, and I watch a flock of starlings gather on a wired fence opposite, then take off and in formation swoop down on a nearby field, no doubt in search of their wormy supper.

The Oxfordshire countryside just south of Napton

Day 36, Friday the 1st of August

I set off at 8:55am, and proceed very slowly, determined to understand every turn of this isolated patch of traditional English countryside.

A year ago I came this way, up from the Thames, and the few photographs from all those I took on the trip, worthy of turning into a painting, came from this stretch of the canal. I want to locate exactly where I took a couple of them. I am also inquisitive to locate the potential crossing point of HS2, which will obviously have a detrimental effect, both visual and sonic, on this section of the canal. There are some signs, and the point is located as just a hundred yards east of bridge 128.

I pass under bridge 130 of this contour hugging canal at 10:03am. The first stop I make back in relative civilisation is the Wharf at Fenny Compton which I reach at 11:12am. The pub has food, is selling gifts and local fresh vegetables, I stop for just a half and a packet of chilli nuts and relax in the pleasant canalside garden. There is a laundrette, but it is clear that the facilities won't be clear for an hour or so.

I set off towards the Fenny Compton tunnel at 11:45. This 'tunnel' was originally made by the 'cut and cover' technique, and now is just a cutting. Near the far end, trees, silt, and a possible land slip, have made it only just passable. This cut is followed by a slowly winding river-like section with nice moorings, each with its own decent sized square plot of land. This is on the hill overlooking Cropedy.

I reach the first downhill lock at 1pm, and am soon through the few locks down into this welcoming and connected community, emerging through the fender maker's lock. A Merlin like figure, the fender maker is sat there in a beautiful garden, with posters for a psychedelic revival band on the window of a caravan.

In a few days time the yearly Cropedy festival, kept going by the enthusiastic remains of the band 'Fairport Convention', is due to start, but it appears that there is music in the pubs in the village as well. In spite of the imminent festival there is a free two day mooring spot right in the centre of the village, which I take. The great thing about a canal boat is if you like somewhere, you can live there, immediately, no bookings required.

I walk to the Kings Arms, in a row of terraced cottages, to investigate, but discover that there is nothing on tonight. The landlord says that it is to give the neighbours a rest. This centre of the village pub has a stage out of the back, and a music shop in the pub. I decide to 'up stakes' and proceed to the countryside of lower Cropredy to moor for the night. It starts to rain.

The Oxfordshire countryside north of Cropedy

Day 37. Saturday the 2nd of August

I realise that it is a good opportunity to make a visit home to check on everything.
It is calm, but a bit damp. I am off early at 6:15am, and run the three locks down to Banbury to moor just past the bend with a

house with many animals – donkeys, dogs and ducks, on the edge of town.

A short walk to the station, and I am home in just two and a half hours via a change at Reading. Tired, I mow the lawn; and deal with the post and emails.

Day 38, Sunday the 3rd of August

A quiet Sunday at home, I do little, and I am exhausted. It is strange that when on the boat, I am rarely tired, I sleep well, and have energy. When I go home after being on the boat for some time, I am usually completely tired out.

I check to see who is playing at the second pub in Cropredy, it is a blues guitar player called Paul Rose.

Day 39, Monday the 4th of August

It takes me from 9:25am to 12:30pm to travel back to Banbury. I walk around town and do some shopping then go back to the boat, which is fine.

At 2 pm I set off with the intention of mooring at a spot in the centre of town, and stopping at the nearby boatyard, I get 18 litres of fuel. The stick level goes from 15.3cm to 18.1 cm, and a calculation using my recalibration of 7.2 litres per cm, indicates its own estimate of the additional fuel at 20 litres – a reasonable agreement.

I re-moor in the centre of town, and do a longer walk around town including a visit to an impressively large and well stocked Morrisons on the outskirts.

The centre of Banbury

It is quite a hike, and my swollen ankle is not too happy. Back on board, I have Paella for supper, and then walk the three miles or so up the canal back to Cropedy and the Bracenose Arms.

Paul Rose is playing accompanied by just a drummer and bass guitarist. He is indeed a guitar impresario, and plays many old standards like 'House of the Rising Sun' and 'All Along the Watchtower'. I record the event on a tiny pocket video camera. After the end of the evening, and after three pints of Adnam's Broadside, I decide it is wiser to get a taxi back to the boat. The Lithuanian taxi driver takes me back to the centre of Banbury, with some indecision about the route.

Day 40, Tuesday the 5th of August

It is rainy. My hangover is not as bad as deserved. Broadside is a good ale. I set off at 9:40am. Delayed by other boats, I finally clear the town swing bridge at 10:15am.

Away from the scant suburbs of Banbury, I am under the M40 by 10:40, then out of Grants lock at 11:14am. I continue to head south.

The Oxfordshire countryside south of Banbury

Eventually I come to Somerton lock. This is the deepest lock on the Oxford canal. It is at an idyllic spot with a beautiful lock keepers cottage. Just above the lock is a perfect mooring place for travellers coming north up the canal.

Once in the past I arrived here going north on my own late on a summers evening. I thought to myself: "Through the lock, then a perfect restful evening moored above". I set the boat in motion, grabbed the rope, and walked up the steps to the lock in preparation for a 'roped through' passage, where you control the boat from the safety of the side of the lock.

To my demise, the boat stopped half way in, jammed by the lower gate that had got some sort of detritus behind it, stopping it from opening fully. No worry, I thought, I will walk down and pull the boat out.

No way, it just wouldn't budge, no matter how hard or from what angle I tugged.

"Well then", I said to myself, " I'll just get onto the boat and do what I can from there, I can even push the gate and have the engine and prop help". Unfortunately, the boat was out of reach: too far in, and too far down to be boarded.

I was beginning to panic – dark was approaching and I didn't even have access to my shelter and home. To my amazement, an unexpected boat arrived above the lock and kindly helped me out of this predicament by pushing the gate beam as hard as possible, whilst I tugged the boat into the lock.

So I remember this episode as I approach the lock this year from above, There is a queue. One boat coming up complains about a tight lower gate. With so many helpers around, the thought of potential trouble clears from my mind until it is actually me and 'Moonstone' inside the lock.

The lock has been drained, the lower gate opened, but to my consternation, again there isn't enough room for me to clear the lock exit.

We all ponder the problem. What is stopping the lock gate from opening fully? I have an idea that something is fouling the base of the gate. I get an extended boat hook, and pummel the underwater area. It is muddy, and feels like piled up fine gravel. Suddenly something gives way. I keep prodding, then those above pull the gate open again and express relief, as suddenly the gate opens just a little more, and I am freed once more from the grips of Somerton lock.

Tomorrow I have arranged to meet an old work acquaintance at Lower Heyford. I reach the road swing bridge no 205 and moor there at 5:12pm in spite of the rather gloomy light, because there seems to be nobody around to help me operate the swing bridge.

Bankside wild flowers

Day 41, Wednesday the 6th of August

I get up early, and take the boat under the swing bridge held open by some helpful passing walkers. I find a much nicer spot to moor, near the station, and clear up to await my guest.

It is over thirty years since I last met Peter Eastty whom I worked with at my second job, nearly forty years ago, at the Cricklewood based 'R&D' section of Electronic Music Studios.

EMS made early electronic music synthesisers. This was at the time of 'Switched-on Bach' and the later Pink Floyd albums. Peter was, and still is a brilliant digital electronics designer. His project for EMS called Vocom, far ahead of its time, was to design and make two digital 'machines' to analyse and synthesise sounds in real time.

I recognise Peter as he steps along the platform. The hair is less and lighter, as is mine! The voice is much the same as it was. It turns out that between bouts of electronic design, he also indulged in a passion for the canals, and had regular jobs moving hire boats from one end of the country to the other during the slack winter season.

We proceed at a constant slow pace, tackling the locks with deliberation. Lunch consists mainly of beer. On return from lunch, one of the mooring cleats hooked around the galvanised rail of the canal bank has become inextricably locked to it. It seems so simple, like a Christmas metal puzzle. You are even allowed to cheat – use a club hammer to try to tap it to a position where it will release. Neither of us can solve this puzzle, so the cleat is left there to provide a mooring point, or possibly just frustration, to whoever comes across it next.

Peter has since designed top of the range digital audio circuits for professional studio equipment and mobile phones. We chat about our projects and lives through the intervening years. He now seems happy and at peace with the world. Reaching the outskirts of Oxford, I decide to take the earlier of two routes from the Oxford canal into the river Thames. This is called Duke's Cut., and I like it because it travels through a windy hinterland into the upper Thames. There is a glorious blue sky, and the air has been cleared by the recent rain. We reach the first lock on the Thames. With a beautifully kept lock and garden the lock keeper comes to meet us and manually closes the huge lock gates, pulling the far one shut with a giant boat hook, and winding open the lock paddles with giant helm wheels. Peter decides to get a Taxi back home from a nearby famous restaurant called the Trout where I drop him off at 6pm.

One more lock, I catch the lock keeper just before he goes off for the day, then I am out onto Port Meadow with its wide vista, wild horses, drinking cattle, geese and evening walkers, past the out of town allotments to moor at Hinksey just above Osney lock. This area, formerly a working class part of Oxford, has now gone 'nouveau-riche'. The pub is now a packed bistro. I am very hungry but I don't want crowds. What I really want is a good curry. With the help of my smartphone, I locate a recommended nearby Indian restaurant, and get a tandoori chicken masalla and a peshwari nan bread, stuffed with almond paste, to take back to the boat.

Day 42, Thursday the 7th of August

I set off at 8:15 to nearby Osney lock. The lock keeper arrives, and I am out by 8:35am. It is a clear blue sky morning. I am sailing towards the low 25° sun. It's a winding stretch of river through the town. With many new apartments, I think that Oxford is a young person's town.
I pass under the 'Folly' and the 'Head of the River' pubs on the bridge that limits the headroom of boats. Many of the 'shark boats' or 'gin palaces', as they used to be called, are too tall to pass above this point.

Passing the university boat houses and rowers, I sound my claxon to avoid a potential collision. I still wonder why skiff rowers don't have small rear view mirrors attached to their heads or to their rowlocks.

After six weeks on the canal, the freedom given by the width of the river is wonderful. I pass John Ody's boat, next to Sam Dent's 'Element'. John Ody is an ex naval engineer who can mend anything mechanical, whilst Sam's boat requires all of John's skills to keep it afloat.

I am out of 'Iffley' lock at 9:19am, passing under the slender steel bridge by the 'Isis', then under the noisy and reverberant arched girder rail bridge. Past electric pylons, skating along a mirror surface, I am overtaken by a lad kneeling in a shallow canoe and paddling furiously.

Out of Sandford lock at 9:25, I pass a boat called 'Unity', with two men busy catching freshwater crayfish and crabs.

The reeds of the upper Thames

As I reach Abingdon, I take time to fill up from the fast flowing hose by the lock. A talkative old lady with a bicycle wants me to buy a pink woollen mouse with a pink woollen purse in aid of animal welfare. She is eccentric, and so open and friendly, that I am happy to oblige, thinking that I know the young daughter of a friend who would like the present.

As I set off to go through the lock, a narrowboat with an electric drive and a generator problem arrives. He moors just below the lock, and I moor further along at 12:11pm. I go for a walk and have a very tasty lunch of mussels in the 'Nag's Head' on the bridge.

I set off again at 2:35pm, and reach Culham lock at 3:26pm. I am near Didcot power station, which has just lost its famous old cooling towers, and just hasn't yet had the fire in its new cooling towers! Culham Science Centre is home to atomic fusion experiments, and rather than generating any electricity, consumes a vast amount, with its very own set of pylons coming from the power station.

Steamboats near Clifton lock

After Clifton lock, I round the stretch towards Day's lock, the idyllic moorings just above the lock are all taken up. I know a lesser used hidden spot in amongst the trees, and manage to tie up there slightly stung by the nettles at 5:20pm. This relatively untouched part of the river has a view south over an ancient hill fort – Wittenham Clumps, and on the north bank there is an ancient Roman Encampment with significant barrows.

Sunset is always a 'next to nature' moment here, spoilt a bit by the low flying helicopters returning to their base at RAF Benson.

I estimate the time for me to return home now at about five days, i.e. the 12th of August.

Day 43, Friday the 8th of August

Off at 9:30, through Day's Lock.

I leave my kitchen waste in the rubbish bin area just below the lock is. Like the sparse water points, you have to look out for them, and there are only just enough.

Round the abrupt left hand turn between the hill to the clumps and the Roman settlement, then after a relatively straight section, the river winds to and fro past the billionaires' houses at Crowmarsh Gifford. Through here at 10:30am, then pass through another straight section and under Shillingford bridge at 10:37am.

Out of Benson Lock at 11:12am, I moor at Wallingford, just above the bridge on the north side, away from the town at 11:30.

I shop at Waitrose, then doze for a while, there is a little rain. I am off again downstream, under the arched stone bridge at 4:25pm.

Eventually under the Brunel railway bridge, at 5:25pm I pass the Beetle and Wedge at Moulsford. This riverside restaurant had a good reputation, but had slid downhill. I am happy to say that it now looks popular and well looked after again.

At 5:51pm I moor above Cleeve lock in open land opposite another 'gastro' pub – The Leathern Bottle. I loop the stern rope around a convenient wooden post, so I only need a mooring pin for the bow line.

Day 44, Saturday the 9th of August

Off at 9:30am, and I fill up with water at Cleeve lock. I am through the lock at 9:48am. Four Canada geese are flying in formation at high speed, and only a few feet up, as they wind down the river,

I am through Goring lock at 10:04am. Past more billionaire's houses, the river makes a left hand turn, under another Brunel railway bridge, and out into open fields with clear breezy sky and sunlight sparkling off the choppy water.

I pass Beale Park Zoo at 10:43am, I have moored here in the past, once next to a wasps nest in the bank! Today there is a huge dark military like object moored at the edge. In the style of a German submarine or 'U'-boat it has its name 'VALHALLA' inscribed in large black gothic letters along the side of its dark grey-brown slightly gilded hull, along with 'KB637'. It is nearly as big as a canal boat can be, some seventy foot long by eleven foot wide. It follows and passest me down towards Pangbourne lock where I get a chance to speak to its owner. He is German, his wife is English. This is the second boat that they have had custom built by a boatyard up in Stockton- on -Tees. They live on it full time. I am out of Pangbourne lock at 11:32, and I wave goodbye to the submarine that has decided to moor again just one patch down.

Submarine style tubby boat 'Valhalla'

I am through Mapledurham lock at 12:09pm, with its nearby preserved period mill house, then after the long open stretch past the park and riverside houses, I moor in the centre of Reading by the recreation ground, downstream of the stone town bridge at 1:26pm. I go and explore the less commercial side of the town on the north of the river. Back to the boat, and get some more diesel, and carry on down through the town lock at 5:20pm.

By 6:20pm I am moored just below Sonning lock in a much more rural location. I have a 'half' in the Bull – accessible by an ancient footpath through the grounds of St Andrews church. My mother lived here from the age of twenty one and the start of the 1940-44 war, away from the bombing of London. By the river is still the hotel where she had her twenty first birthday party.

In the tall trees opposite there is a cacophony from a myriad of green parquets.

Day 45, Sunday the 10th August.

I have arranged to meet a friend I haven't seen for a while for lunch near Henley, so despite the darkness and rain, which has eased off a little bit, I set off at 7:40am.

Between Sonning and Shiplake there are a couple of islands which can provide a brilliant summers evening mooring place. As I approach the first of these, I spy what looks like a giant orange inflatable balloon in the water. Is this marking some wreck or sand bank?

As I near the object things get stranger: I see goggled swimmers in wet suits swimming ferociously towards the balloon. Is this an anti terrorist operation? Or is it just a hardening up session for some SAS brigade? I am still a couple of hundred yards from the object when I hear paddling from behind, and a man in a canoe says I should cut my engine and moor to the right.

I know this is impossible with shallow water and overhanging alder trees. I feel insulted, so I take a more commanding tone. I say I am slowing right down to a tick over, and that it is impossible to moor, and that I am quite aware of the swimmers, and certainly don't want them tangled up in my propeller, and ask what's going on anyway.

To my surprise, he takes on a more reasonable tone. He explains that he is a house master in a local public school, and they are having a swimming race! I look carefully and see now that the swimmers are young. One of the dozen or so is definitely lagging behind, now that they have reached the balloon and are on the homeward strait. I can now see the grassy slope and riverside plain from which the event is being organised. Many more pupils, and no doubt, house masters are stood watching the swimmers. It has been drizzling, not that that would effect the swimmers, but it is intensifying into a downpour, and further into a deluge.

Suddenly there is an intense flash of light, and I see a fork of lightening has struck only some tens of yards behind them. There is an intense bang which has frightened the umpire. He shouts to the swimmers through a loud hailer to abandon the race and swim back to base. Luckily nothing worse happens. I am left alone on the river, its surface now made opaque by the intensity of rain.

As I get to Shiplake lock the rain abates. I am out of Shiplake by 8:38am, past the most expensive riverside 'sheds' in the world, then past the hamlet of beautiful riverside houses and large trees, round the large open turn of the river to Marsh lock. Then it is a short distance to the recreation ground in Henly where I moor at 9:45am.

Finally, my friend turns up and he drives us to a good pub restaurant, the Frog at Skirmett, where we chat over lunch and, now that the rain has truly abated, do a short walk around the hill above the pub. I return back to the boat. Moonstone is well tied to the mooring rings.

Day 46, Monday the 11th of August

I set off at 8:40am, and have passed under the town bridge just ten minutes later.

Temple Island

I am heading down the 'long straight mile' where the rowing boats of the Henley regatta raced just a few weeks earlier. I pass Temple Island at 9:10am where the races are started, and am through Hambledon lock by 9:33am.

I pass Westfield Farm at 9:55am. Here the banks of a large flood plain provide a beautiful mooring place. Mooring fees are collected by the farm who own the land. Although they are very meticulous in collecting their dues, it is one place on the Thames that is worth it, with the possibilities of open air picnic barbecues with a long view of the setting sun, and no sight of roads or towns.

I am past Medmenham Abbey at 10:00am, its medieval remains preserved and turned into a conference centre. After which is 'Black Boy' island, taken over by myriads of both white and Canada geese, then past the high cliffs with the old secret wartime secret operations headquarters, now a luxury hotel, perched on its edge. Here reconnaissance flight photographs of Germany were analysed.

I go through Hurley lock at 10:35am, it is a short hop to Temple lock, exiting at 10:52 and down the long strait past Bisham Abbey to Marlow with its impressive Victorian iron suspension bridge.

Bisham Abbey

I am through Marlow lock at 11:20am, and under the bypass bridge at 11:25am.
Here I have a race with two large canoes full of furiously paddling, life jacketed teenagers, as we pass a square turreted mock castle riverside house.

I pass Bourne End at 11:47am then past the Bounty Inn, stopping for a break. Setting off under Bourne End railway bridge, I remember this area back in January. The houses on the starboard side between the Bounty and the railway bridge were flooded and effectively stranded between the river and a huge lake of floodwater behind. The whole of the Cookham flood plain was used as a run off to try to keep the river flow under control.

On the left northerly bank opposite Cookham are some very large houses. I count twenty bedrooms in one of them. I am past the bridge and the Ferry pub by 12:06pm to turn left into the lock cut.

Out of the lock and I am heading south below the stately home of Cliveden overlooking the 'reach' from its hillside perch. This house and gardens, now a posh hotel, was the site of John Profumo's affair with Christine Keeler which led to the downfall of Harold Macmillan's conservative and establishment government in the sixties.

At the bottom of the reach the river divides. To the left, the new 'Jubilee River', barred from navigation, has been cut to try to alleviate flooding in Maidenhead. At the end of the reach is Boulters lock, which I am through at 12:57pm.

Under Maidenhead road bridge at 1:06pm, and under the widest span Brunel railway bridge, past the celebrities homes including that of the disgraced Rolf Harris, towards Bray, home of the Roux brothers restaurant, The Waterside Inn, and Heston Blumenthal's Fat Duck.

Out of Bray lock at 1:44pm, and past Monkey Island with its hotel and infamous back cut which is navigable, but can be treacherous because currents at its upstream end can push a boat onto both rocks or strand it in the shallows. I have been there!

I pass the impressive Victorian Gothic Oakley Court hotel, then round a turn and through Windsor lock by the race course at 2:30pm

A flock of beady eyed Turkish geese fly past up the river.

Under the railway bridge, I turn, after a DuckTour boat passes. These amphibious vehicles used to take tourists across the Thames in London until one of them caught alight. I moor on the inside of the town side islands at 3pm.

Day 47, Tuesday the 12th of August

Today I have invited a friend, her three year old daughter, and cousin who is visiting from abroad, to spend the day on the boat. She lives near Shepperton, and so they will come by train, and with luck, I should be able to get to Sunbury-on-Thames to drop them off by evening.

Windsor has two railway stations; both are the termini for small branch lines. One runs from Slough at the western end of the town, and one from Feltham via Datchet at the eastern end. There is a pleasant, distinctively Victorian, feel about the railway and station.

I meet my guests and we set off around the island, and downstream with a grand view of the castle, then under the town bridge with Eton on the left. We reach the town lock which is slower but more interesting than usual, since we have to operate the electric controls ourselves. The lock keeper is having his lunch break.

We drift on down past the tree lined edge of the Royal park on the right, and Datchet on the left, where the fibreglass hire boats with Royal names lay in wait for their holidaymakers.

Then we are through Old Windsor lock and onto the stretch of the Thames past Runnymead where the Magna Carta was 'sealed' in June 1215, uniting the barons of England under king John.

Past a bend, and there is the January flooded Wraysbury on the left. Here the damage is still apparent. One riverside bungalow has a steel girder platform through its base in readiness for a crane lift, so that an extra few feet can be added to its foundations. Another bungalow seems to have been almost completely ripped apart by a gas explosion.

We pass through Bell Weir lock and under the wide smoothly curved arches of the M25 bridge. Now we are back in the vicinity of London – soon to pass under the old stone bridge into Staines.

Past Laleham, then through Chertsy, Penton-Hook and, Shepperton locks.

Below Shepperton lock there is a choice of routes around a large island. We take the scenic route past Shepperton village, rather than the Desborough Cut.

Under the new Walton Bridge and down through Sunbury lock to moor in the weir pool by the road, and drop my passengers off. We have been relatively lucky with the weather during the day, but now the heavens open. I wait with my group under some shelter until their bus arrives, then I have a swift half and a packet of crisps in the pub before returning back to the boat.

It is a strange feeling being back relatively close to home again.

Day 48, Wednesday the 13th of August

Maybe I can get home today, it is early, and I am only a short hop from Teddington lock, the entry to the tidal part of the Thames. The tide times indicate that it may be towards the end of the afternoon before I can proceed down to Thames lock Brentford, the entry point back into the canal network.

I am off at 8:10am. A skiff is rowing furiously towards me without looking where he is going. I let out a squawk from my newly renovated claxon which averts a collision.

Stalwart stoics of waterside bungalows drinking their morning coffee share this blue sky sunlit shimmering river. I get a wave from the arm of a skeleton held by a jockular old man at the bottom of his garden.

I am past Taggs and Ash island just above Hampton Court. I replenish my water tank at the fast hose at Hampton lock, then through at 9:22am.

Then under the wide and majestic bridge and past Hampton Court Palace, then pass the island at Thames Ditton at 9:39am.

This was the scene of a mishap several years back. With exuberance, on returning from another boat trip, I reached here and tried to cross a small gap between the two islands only to find the boat firmly wedged in the mud. It took many attempts to get pulled out, finally successfully by a powerful sixty five foot narrow boat the next day!

Just past here the river swings round a bend to the strait leading towards Kingston. I pass the yellow and blue stepped style Dutch barge 'Ark Newvaux' at 9:45am, then under Kingston bridge at 10:10am,

I finally reach Teddington lock by 10:39am, after passing the persistent local boat squatting community including 'Hui' and a very top heavy barge.

As I have time to spare, I see my friends Lesley and Phil, who live nearby.

Back at the lock, I consult with the lock keeper about passage down to Brentford. I also try to ring Brentford lock. I get no reply. Neither does another boat waiting for the same passage. Finally I am released onto the tidal Thames at 4:25, following two other boats that are making faster headway than mine.

It is a struggle because it is about a two hours before high tide, and I am fighting the stream coming up the river. I have known it far worse, and I get to Thames lock Brentford at 5:55pm.

There is no sign of a lock keeper, my heart is low, maybe he has gone off for the evening. By now the tide is high, so Moonstone is up high and I stand a chance of seeing any signs of life in the central control room on the lock. As I slowly approach the lock, a figure finally appears, not welcoming, but with an open palm held up.

"You can't come into the lock until I have seen your licence" shouts the man. At that moment the engine judders as a huge piece of rope fouls the propeller. I frantically reverse the engine, but the rope doesn't want to come free, there are clouds of blue smoke, and I am drifting towards a collision with the lock gates. Finally the rope is gone, and finally the man opens the gates. I am annoyed by his attitude. He is hired apparently by the Canal and River Trust as a stand–in from a private company. Apparently CRT cannot now afford a proper lock keeper. I feel there is a safety issue with his lack of communication with Teddington lock.

I am through the key operated half-tide lock then through 'Clitheroe's lock'. I pass some other boats moored just past a Victorian cast iron footbridge. I recognise the brown colour scheme on one of the boats. It is a hire boat on its way back to Willowtree Marina. I negotiate another lock in Brentford Park to finally moor at 8:11pm, at the foot of the Hanwell flight behind several live-on boats.

Day 49, Thursday the 14th of August

I am up and off at 8am. Ready to tackle the lock flight on my own, I am soon through two of the eight, when I spy the hire boat back in the first lock. I wait for them to catch up, and together we manage the flight. I point out the local sights – the wall at the back of the Hanwell aylum, and the bridge where the road passes over the canal, itself twenty foot above the railway. We manage the flight in a record 2h 10m. They are an extended white South African family, and are all charming.

Shortly after the final lock, and passing through the south east of Southall, we all decide to stop for a celebration at a pub by the canal. The landlady has only just arrived, but I explain that I have a hire boat full of people nearby and she opens the place up.

It's a rather dingy place, smelling of stale beer and incense, but outside there is a long table where we sit and have some lunch.

At 12:30pm I bid farewell and head on, past Tescos at Bull's bridge where I head right for the final spur up to Willowtree, where I moor at 1:30pm.

I ring for a taxi to take me the three miles home. After a long wait, the Ghanaian driver arrives. He is smiling, but unsettling, and tells me about his life in Africa, with pirate runs of contraband petrol, and cutting into pipelines. I finally get back home at 3pm.

Richard Monkhouse, October 2014

The End

89

www.ingramcontent.com/pod-product-compliance
Lightning Source LLC
Chambersburg PA
CBHW042338150426
43195CB00001B/31